Date: 03/01/12

CHINESE NEW YEAR

BY ANN HEINRICHS · ILLUSTRATED BY BENREI HUANG

Published in the United States of America by The Child's World®
PO Box 326 • Chanhassen, MN 55317-0326
800-599-READ • www.childsworld.com

ACKNOWLEDGMENTS
The Child's World®: Mary Berendes, Publishing Director

Editorial Directions, Inc.: E. Russell Primm, Editorial Director; Katie Marsico, Managing Editor; Judith Shiffer,
Assistant Editor; Caroline Wood and Rory Mabin, Editorial Assistants; Susan Hindman, Copy Editor and
Proofreader; Elizabeth Nellums, Rory Mabin, Ruth Martin, and Caroline Wood, Fact Checkers; Tim Griffin/
IndexServ, Indexer

The Design Lab: Kathleen Petelinsek, Design and Page Production

LIBRARY OF CONGRESS CATALOGING-IN-PUBLICATION DATA
Heinrichs, Ann.
  Chinese New Year / by Ann Heinrichs; illustrated by Benrei Huang.
    p. cm. — (Holidays, festivals, & celebrations)
  Includes index.
  ISBN 1-59296-572-5 (library bound : alk. paper) 1.Chinese New Year—Juvenile literature. I. Huang, Benrei ill.
II. Title. III. Series.
  GT4905.H45 2006
  394.261—dc22   2005025681

TABLE OF CONTENTS

CHAPTER ONE

GUNG HAY FAT CHOY!

Bright red banners hang in every doorway. A fierce dragon snakes through the streets. Firecrackers crackle and pop. It's Chinese New Year!

Chinese New Year is a joyful holiday. It's a time to make all things fresh and new. People exchange wishes for good luck and happiness. Would you like to learn the Chinese New Year greeting? Just say, *"Gung hay fat choy!"*

Is that a dragon in the street? It must be time for Chinese New Year!

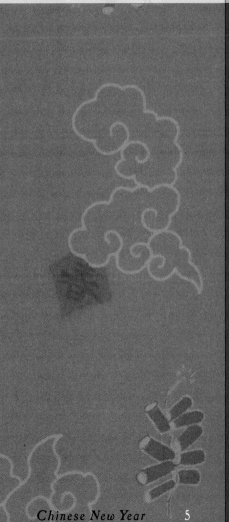

Another way of spelling the Chinese New Year greeting is Gong Xi Fa Cai!

CHAPTER TWO

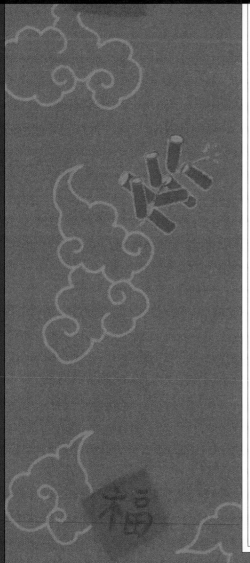

NEW YEAR IN A NEW LAND

China is a faraway land. It's in Asia, far across the Pacific Ocean. But many Chinese people live in the United States. Some came as **immigrants**. Others are children or grandchildren of immigrants.

Chinese people brought many **customs** with them. One is celebrating Chinese New Year. It's the biggest festival of the year!

Many cities have a Chinese neighborhood. In some places, it's called Chinatown. Chinese shops and restaurants line the streets. And delicious smells fill the air.

Would you like to see a Chinese New Year parade? Just visit your local Chinatown!

Your local Chinatown is the perfect place to take in Chinese culture.

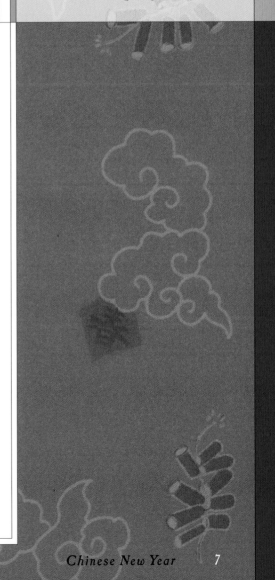

Chinese New Year is often called the Spring Festival.

CHAPTER THREE

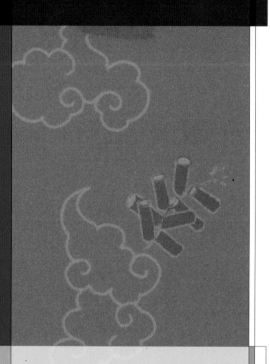

An old Chinese belief says that the second day of the New Year is the birthday of all dogs. People should be kind to dogs that day.

WHEN IS CHINESE NEW YEAR?

The date of Chinese New Year depends on the moon!

The Chinese calendar is a lunar calendar. That means it follows the stages of the moon. Each month begins at the new moon. That's when we can't see the moon at all. Why? Because Earth is blocking it from the sun's light.

Chinese New Year is the first day of the first month. On the Western calendar, it falls sometime between January 20 and February 20. That's when you'll see the dragon parade!

Want to see a dragon parade? Check out a Chinese calendar and mark the first day of the first month.

CHAPTER FOUR

WHY A DRAGON?

Dragons appear in many **ancient** Chinese **legends.** One legend about the New Year's dragon goes like this: Long ago, a village was gripped with fear. In the nearby forest lived a terrible dragon. He came out on the night before New Year's. He swept through the village, swallowing people up.

One New Year's Eve, an old man appeared. The dragon, he said, was afraid of loud noises. It also feared bright lights and the color red.

Quickly, the villagers prepared for the dragon's visit. They banged drums and gongs. They lit big fires. And they hung up red decorations. Sure enough, the dragon ran away!

How did Chinese villagers scare the dragon away? According to legend, they used bright lights, loud noises, and the color red.

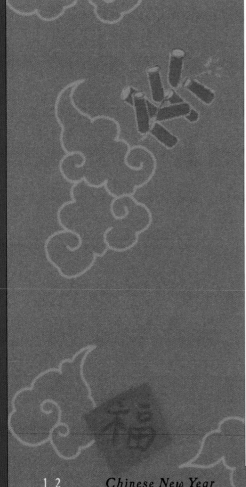

Nian is the name of the dragon in the legend. Nian is also the Chinese word for "year."

Now the dragon appears in every Chinese New Year parade. And people still know how to scare him away. With noisy firecrackers, lanterns, and red decorations!

Red decorations, firecrackers, and lanterns are part of the Chinese New Year celebration.

CHAPTER FIVE

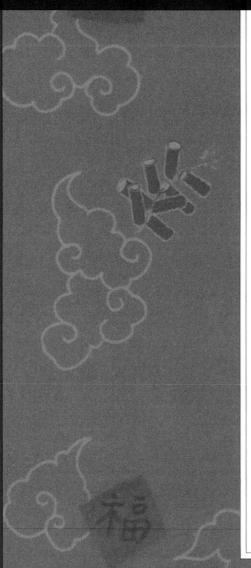

PREPARING THE HEART

Chinese New Year celebrates more than the passing of time. It brings the promise of hope and joy. It's a time to lay aside old ways and welcome the new.

New clothes are one way to make a fresh start.

People prepare their hearts for this day. They clear up any bad feelings with others. They want to start the New Year as friends.

Bills are paid before the New Year, too. This creates peace and **goodwill.** People get haircuts and buy new clothes. All must be fresh for the New Year!

Some people get haircuts in preparation for Chinese New Year.

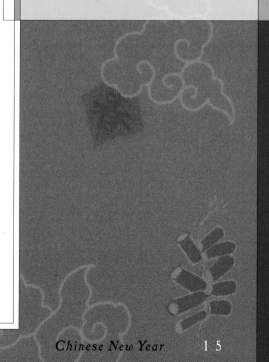

FOLK BELIEFS FOR NEW YEAR'S DAY

- *Don't sweep the house. Then good luck cannot be swept away.*
- *Don't use a knife or scissors. You may cut off your good luck.*
- *Don't cry, or you will cry all year.*

CHAPTER SIX

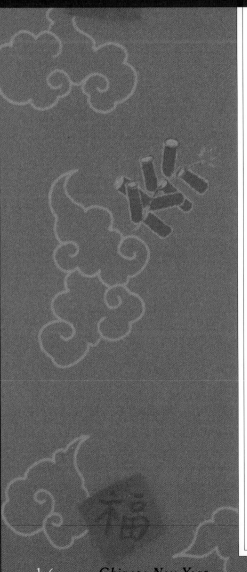

PREPARING THE HOME

The home must be ready for the New Year! As the day approaches, people clean their homes. They're sweeping away any bad luck. That makes it easier for good luck to come in.

Spring **couplets** are hung up as decorations. Each one is a lucky saying or a happy wish. They're written on red paper with gold trim.

People remember the Kitchen God, too. A week before New Year, the Kitchen God leaves the home. He will tell the Jade Emperor about the family. That night, people leave sweet foods out for the Kitchen God. Then he will say only sweet things!

Families leave sweet offerings for the Kitchen God
a week before Chinese New Year.

The Jade Emperor is the king of heaven, or the king of the gods.

CHINESE NEW YEAR

You'll find whenever the
New Year comes
The Kitchen God will want
some plums.
The girls will want some
flowers new;
The boys will want
firecrackers, too.
A new felt cap will please
papa,
And a sugar cake for dear
mama.

—Chinese nursery rhyme

Vases of flowers are placed around the house in preparation for Chinese New Year. They stand for rebirth and new growth. There are bowls of oranges and tangerines, too. They stand for good luck and wealth.

CHAPTER SEVEN

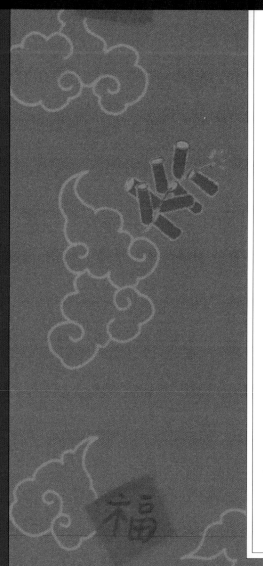

THE FAMILY COMES TOGETHER

On New Year's Eve, the whole family shares a hearty dinner. One dish is a whole fish. It stands for togetherness and plentifulness. Long, uncut noodles are served, too. They stand for a long life.

That night, all the lights are kept on. At midnight, fireworks light up the sky and firecrackers explode. This scares away bad luck!

In the morning, each child receives a Lai-See envelope. It's a lucky red envelope with money inside.

Later that day, people visit relatives and friends.

They share a Tray of Togetherness. This dish holds eight sweet foods. Each one has a special meaning for the New Year.

The Tray of Togetherness contains eight different sweet foods.

THE TRAY OF TOGETHERNESS

Candied melon—growth and good health

Red melon seeds—joy, happiness, and truth

Lychee nuts—close family ties

Kumquats—wealth

Coconut—togetherness

Peanuts—long life

Longnan—many good sons

Lotus seeds—many children

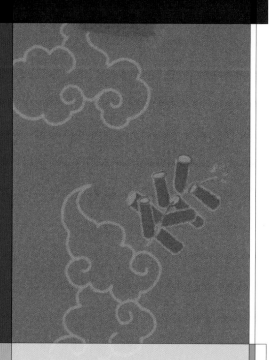

CHAPTER EIGHT

FIFTEEN DAYS OF JOY

New Year is a long festival in China and some other Asian lands. The celebrations last for fifteen days!

Each day of the New Year brings special activities. On the fifteenth day, the full moon rises. That's the day of the Lantern Festival.

At night, people parade through the streets carrying lanterns. Young men do dragon dances, and firecrackers go off. At last, the New Year season comes to an end.

In the United States, only a few Chinatowns celebrate the Lantern Festival.

The Lantern Festival marks the end of Chinese New Year.

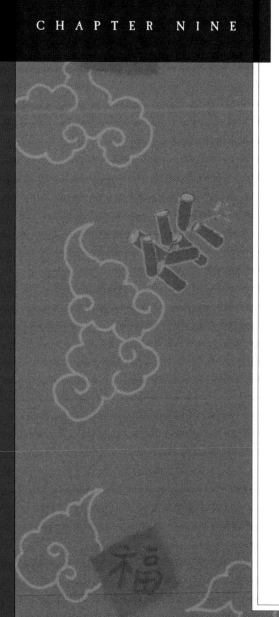

CHAPTER NINE

ANIMALS OF THE CHINESE CALENDAR

E ach year in the Chinese calendar is matched with an animal. Twelve animals are used altogether. Every twelve years, the animal list begins again. Suppose you were born in 1998. That was the Year of the Tiger!

The Chinese calendar features twelve animals, including the tiger.

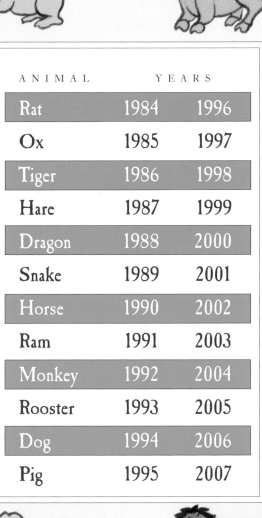

ANIMAL	YEARS	
Rat	1984	1996
Ox	1985	1997
Tiger	1986	1998
Hare	1987	1999
Dragon	1988	2000
Snake	1989	2001
Horse	1990	2002
Ram	1991	2003
Monkey	1992	2004
Rooster	1993	2005
Dog	1994	2006
Pig	1995	2007

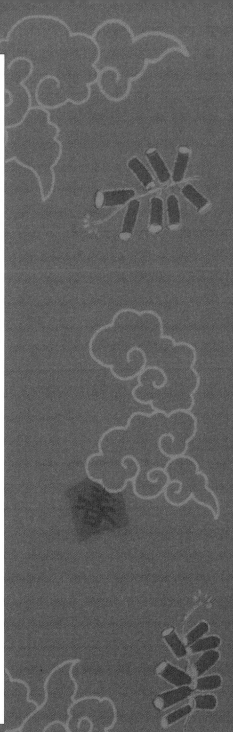

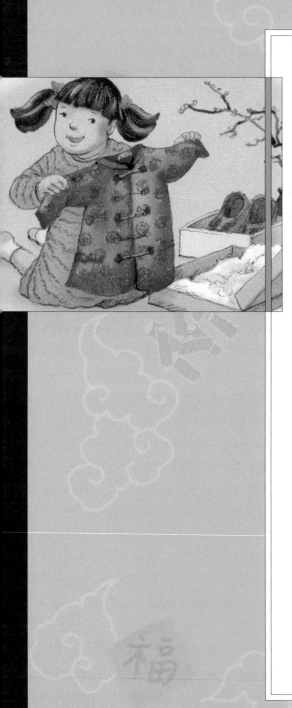

Joining in the Spirit of Chinese New Year

· Do you know a Chinese American? Ask him or her about family celebrations for Chinese New Year.

· Is there a Chinese neighborhood in your community? Find out if it holds a Chinese New Year parade. If so, go and watch the exciting dragon dance!

· Visit a Chinese restaurant. Red holiday decorations may be hanging up. Ask the workers which animal goes with this year.

· Write spring couplets with happy wishes. Copy them onto red paper and hang them on the walls.

· Make a new start for Chinese New Year. Clean your room and give old toys away. Get in touch with an old friend.

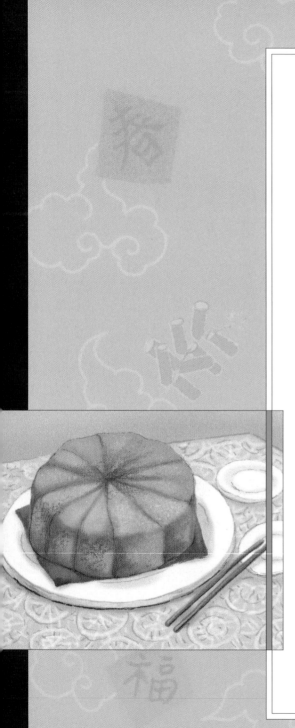

Making Nian Gao
(Chinese New Year Cake)

Ingredients:

3 eggs
2 cups brown sugar
3 cups glutinous rice flour
   (available at most Asian
   markets)
2 ½ cups milk
1 tablespoon vanilla

½ cup chopped dates
2 teaspoons baking soda
⅓ cup vegetable oil
Cooking spray or a stick of
   butter/margarine
Sesame seeds

Directions:

Preheat the oven to 350 degrees Fahrenheit.* Lightly grease a tube
or bundt pan with cooking spray or a little butter (or margarine). In
a large mixing bowl, beat together the eggs and sugar. Slowly stir in
the rice flour and milk. Mix the ingredients until they are completely
blended. Next, slowly add the vanilla, dates, baking soda, and vegetable
oil. Pour the mixture into the greased pan and bake for fifty minutes.
Allow the cake to cool for fifteen minutes before removing it from the
pan. Finally, sprinkle the top with sesame seeds. Share with twelve to
sixteen people while you welcome the New Year!

   Special Note: Be sure to follow directions about stirring in the
ingredients *slowly.* Nian Gao is a very dense cake, and this will keep
extra air from getting into the mixture.

*Have an adult help you operate the oven.

Making a Circle Snake

*No Chinese New Year celebration would be complete without
a snake or two. Here's a fun and easy snake project.*

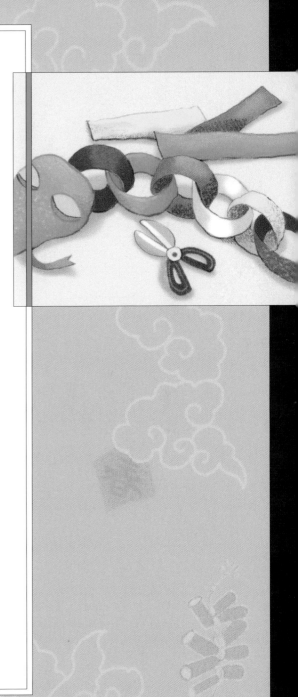

What you need:
Construction paper (4 different colors)
Scissors
Glue

Instructions:
1. Cut twelve 1-inch strips from three different sheets of construction paper.
2. Take one strip of paper and glue the ends so it forms a ring.
3. Put another strip of paper through the ring and glue the ends together. Continue doing this until you've used all the strips of paper and you have a long chain.
4. Draw a snake's head on another sheet of construction paper and cut it out.
5. Glue the head onto the end of your chain.

*Now you're ready to parade your snake through your
house or neighborhood. Happy New Year!*

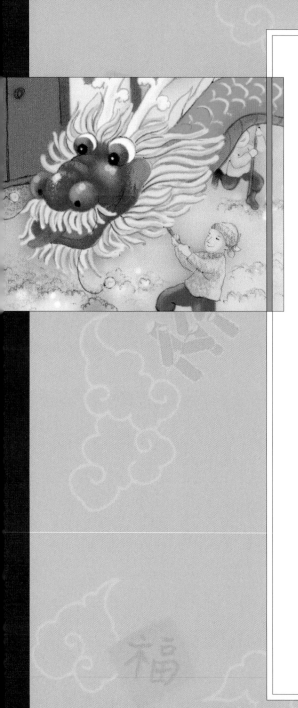

Words to Know

ancient (*AYN-shunt*) very old

couplets (*CUP-lehts*) two-line poems

customs (*CUSS-tums*) ways of doing things

goodwill (*good-WILL*) good feelings between people

immigrants (*IM-uh-grunts*) people who move to another country

legends (*LEJ-undhz*) very old stories

How to Learn More about Chinese New Year

At the Library

Bledsoe, Karen E. *Chinese New Year Crafts.* Berkeley Heights, N.J.: Enslow Publishers, 2005.

Compestine, Ying Chang, and Tungwai Chau (illustrator). *The Runaway Rice Cake.* New York: Simon & Schuster Books for Young Readers, 2001.

Gower, Catherine, and He Zhihong (illustrator). *Long-Long's New Year: A Story about the Chinese Spring Festival.* Boston: Tuttle Publishers, 2005.

Jango-Cohen, Judith, and Jason Chin (illustrator). *Chinese New Year.* Minneapolis: Carolrhoda Books, 2005.

Wong, Janet S., and Yangsook Choi (illustrator). *This Next New Year.* New York: Frances Foster Books, 2000.

On the Web

Visit our home page for lots of links about Chinese New Year:
http://www.childsworld.com/links

NOTE TO PARENTS, TEACHERS, AND LIBRARIANS:
We routinely verify our Web links to make sure they're safe, active sites—so encourage your readers to check them out!

ABOUT THE AUTHOR

Ann Heinrichs lives in Chicago, Illinois. She has written more than two hundred books for children. She loves traveling to faraway places.

ABOUT THE ILLUSTRATOR

Benrei Huang was born and raised in Taiwan and came to live in the United States in 1986. She has illustrated more than twenty-five books for children.

Index